Travel English Dialogues

50 English Conversation Dialogues, ESL

By FAB CHRIS

Copyright 2024 Fab Chris

Table of Contents

TRAVEL BY AIR

Booking a flight (At airline office)
A: Good Morning. Can I help you?
B: Yes. I want to book a one-way flight to London.
A: When do you want to travel?
B: I want to travel on the twenty-second of June.
A: Do you prefer a morning flight at 7 am or an evening flight at 8 pm?
B: I prefer the morning flight.
A: What class do you want?
B: I'd like first-class and window seat
A: That would be 200 pounds.
B: Okay
A: Could I have your name and address, please?
B: Adam Peterson and my address is nr 2 Reagan Street, Warsaw.
A: Done. Remember to confirm this ticket before the departure date.

Useful phrases for booking a flight
Airline ticket clerk :
What airline do you want to travel by?
What city are you travelling to?
Do you want a way or round trip ticket?
First-class, business, or economy class? (What class do you want?)
May I have your passport, please?
What is your destination? / Where are you flying to?
What is your travel date? / When do you want to travel?
What is your date of return?
Would you prefer a morning or night flight?

Traveller :
What flight gets me to Warsaw by 9 p.m.?
When is the next plane to London?
Are seats still available at the 3 o'clock flight to Paris?
Could I book myself on a plane to Warsaw?
Are there any airplanes to Warsaw on Saturdays?
What time do I have to report at the airport?
How much is a first-class ticket?
How much luggage am I allowed to carry?

Changing flight booking (At the airline office)
A: Good morning sir. Can I be of any help?
B: Yes, I need to change my reservation.
A: May I know the reasons for this?
B: Because the starting date of my course in London has been changed.
A: OK. Can I have your name and the departure date?
B: My name is Adam Brown and the departure date is May 2nd.
A: What date do you want to travel to?
B: I would appreciate it if you could change the departure date to June 15th.
A: Let me check if there is an available seat then.
B: Okay.
A: Yes, there is a free seat on the three o'clock flight. Is this ok for you?
B: Yes.
A: I have changed this to June 15th, a three o'clock flight.
B: Thank you.

Useful phrases for changing a flight booking
Airline ticket clerk:
Who is the booking for?
Has the booking been confirmed?
Can I have your name, please?
Why do you want to change this?
May I know your reasons for changing this?
Can L change the departure date to…?
Is there anything else I can help you with?
No problem I will change it.
Let's check if there is an available seat.
You have to pay reservation change fees.
Traveller:
Could you change my departure date?
Can I change my booking?
Is it possible to change my reservation?
Do I have to pay any fees?
I'll appreciate it if you could change this to 1st May.
I come to change the flight reservation I made here.
I have to change my travel plans because of (my child's sickness)

Getting flight information (**At the airport info desk**)
A: Hello. What can I do for you?
B: This is my first time at the airport and I don't know where to start.
A: Where are you flying to? And what time is your plane?
B: I'm flying to London and my flight is at 10 am.
A: OK, you still have two hours. First, you've to check in at that place.
B: What do I do next?
A: When they have checked you in, they will give you a boarding pass to enter.
B: What do I do after that?
A: You've to undergo many checks and controls
B: What checks and controls?
A: Passport control, customs control, and security check before boarding the plane.
B: Thank you very much.

Useful phrases used at the airport info desk

Traveller's questions
Where can I find a beverage and snack vending machine?
Where is the washroom?
Where is the baby care room?
Where are banking services here?
Where is the Polish Airline ticket office?
Where is the luggage claim office?
Where is the left luggage office?
How are many checking-in points at this airport?
Where is the check-in desk for flight BA 234?
What is the check-in time for flight BA 234?
How much will the departure of this plane be delayed?
Where is the car rental stand?
Where do airport hotel buses leave from?
Are there any cash machines at this airport?
Are there any luggage lockers here?
Where can I find a taxi?
Where is the domestic level?
Where is the international level?

Checking in at the airport
A: Good morning. Can I have your air ticket, please?
B: Yes, here you are.
A: You are in business class, which type of seat would you like?
B: Aisle seat, please.
A: Do you have any baggage?
B: Yes, this suitcase, and this small handbag.
A: Put your suitcase on the scale, please.
B: Ok.
 A: It weighs 30 kg. **I'm afraid you have to pay for excess luggage.**
B: How much am I allowed to carry and how much do I pay?
A: You are allowed to carry 25kg only. For the extra 5 kg, you have to
pay $25'
B: Here you go.
A: Here is your boarding pass. Have a nice flight.

Useful phrases for check-in at the airport

Checking in desk clerk :
Where are you flying to?
May I see your ticket?
Can I have your passport and ticket, please?
Do you have a booking reference?
Do you have an e-ticket?
Is this your suitcase?
Do you have any baggage?
How many suitcases have you got?
How many pieces of luggage do you have?
How many bags are you checking in?
Have you got a handbag?
Do you have a carry-on bag?
Could I see your handbag, please?
Would you like a window or aisle seat?
Do you prefer a window or aisle?
Traveller :
How much do I pay for excess luggage?
Can I take this with me?
What is our boarding gate?
Could I have a seat closest to the emergency exit?
What is my flight terminal?

Passport and visa control (at the airport)

A: Hello. May I see your passport?
B: Certainly. Here you go.
A: Is this your first visit to the US?
B: Yes, it is.
A: What is the purpose of your visit?
B: I'm here on vacation.
A: How long are you going to stay?
B: For a month.
A: Where will you stay?
B: At the Hilton Hotel.
A: OK. How much currency have you got?
B: I have only $ 4000
A: Here you are your passport. Have a nice stay.

Useful phrases used at the airport passport control

Passport officer :
Could I see your passport and boarding pass, please?
What is the country of your final destination?
What is the purpose of your visit/trip?
May I have a look at your passport?
Is anybody (else) travelling with you?
Are you travelling alone?
What is your country of residence?
Why are you visiting?
Where will you be staying?
Who will you be visiting?
Do you have any family here in the UK?
How long will you be staying?
How long are you staying?
How long do you plan to stay?
How much money are you bringing?
Is this your first visit to this country?
Have you ever been here before?
Have you visited the country before?
How often do you come to…?
What is your line of work?

Customs control (At the airport)
A: Have you filled and signed a customs clearance form?
B: Yes, I have.
A: Do you have anything to declare?
B: No, I don't.
A: How many pieces of baggage do you have?
B: I have only this travelling bag.
A: Who packed the bag?
B: I did it
A: What do you have in your bag?
B: My clothes and other personal belongings.
A: Can you open your bag, please?
B: Yes, of course.
A: Everything is ok. Have a nice stay.

<u>Useful phrases used at the airport customs control</u>

<u>Custom officer :</u>
Have you got something to declare?
Have you filled and signed customs clearance forms?
What have you got in your suitcase?
Can you open your suitcase, please?
Could you open this bag for me?
Do you have any products made from endangered species?
Did you pack this baggage yourself?
Have you got any objects of art and museum Pieces?
Would you mind opening the suitcase, please?
Did you leave your luggage unattended?
Are you carrying Flammable materials?
Any food items in your bag?
How much are they worth?
You are not allowed to take this out of the country.
Please get ready for customs clearance.
Please get your luggage ready for customs inspection.
Please do this way, if you have nothing to declare.
You have to declare all your valuables.
You can't bring this into this country
You have to pay customs for this.
<u>Traveller:</u>

I have only my personal belongings.
I have only $400 (in currency).
I am here on vacation.

Security check (at the airport)

A: Come over here, please.
B: Yes, sir.
A: Have you got any weapons, sharp objects, or food in your bag?
B: No, I have none of these.
A: Do you have a laptop?
B: No, I don't
A: Empty your pockets and make sure you have no metals.
B: Done. I have taken out my keys and cell phone.
A: Take off your shoes, hat, watch, and belt also.
B: Okay sir.
A: Pack all these items in this plastic tray.
B: Do I have to remove my coat also?
A: Yes. Put your coat, the tray, and your bag on the X-ray machine's conveyor
B: Sure.
A: Now, walk through this metal detector.

<u>Useful phrases used at the airport security check</u>

<u>Security officer :</u>
Are there any knives, guns, or other forbidden items in your bag?
Do you have any mobile phones or laptops?
Please could you put your bag through the X-ray machine?
May I check your wig with a hand scanner?
Do have you a stoma or prosthetic device?
Please take your laptops and phones out of your bag.
Empty your pockets.
Put your keys, belt, and shoes in the tray.
Walk through the metal detector
Please come back and step through the machine again.
Please come here for body scanning.

Shopping at the duty-free shop (at the airport)
A: Hello, can I help you?
B: Yes, I want to buy something for my boyfriend.
A: How about buying this men's gold watch?
B: No. it is too expensive.
A: Well, belts, purses, Whisky, and perfumes are good for men.
B: Can you give me that perfume?
A: Yes, here you are.
B: Great. I love the smell of this perfume. How much is it?
A: It is 80 euros.
B: I'll take it.
A: Can I see your boarding pass?
B: Yes. Here's my boarding card
A: How do you want to pay?
B: I pay cash.

Useful phrases used at the airport duty-free shop
Traveller (buyer):

How many cigarettes am I allowed to buy?
How much alcohol can I buy here?
Which men's perfume do you recommend?
What types of electronics do you sell?
What popular souvenirs do you have?
Where is the cosmetic counter?
Could you gift-wrap them for me?
Can I have this in a tamper-evident bag?
What value of goods can I buy here?
What are your payment options?
Can I pay with traveller's cheque?
What currencies do you accept here?

Duty-free shop clerk:
Are you travelling outside the EU?
Can I see your boarding pass?
How do you want to pay?
Will you pay in cash or by credit card?
Thank you for shopping with us.
Have a safe flight.

Boarding a Plane dialogue

A: Our boarding has been changed from Gate number 5 to Gate 9.
B: Okay, let's go to Gate 9 now.
A: Let's hurry; We have to be there before the boarding time.
B: What time are we boarding the plane?
A: The boarding time is I pm, that's in 10 minutes.
B: Do passengers in first class go on board first?
A: Certainly yes.
B: We are in the economy class, so we still have time.
A: True but we don't have much time.
B: Do you have our boarding cards?
A: Yes, please take your boarding card.
B: Oh, my seat number is 128A And yours?
A: My seat is next to yours.

Useful phrases for on-plane announcements

<u>**On-plane announcements**</u>

Ladies and gentlemen, this is Ba flight 506 boards to…
All the carry-on baggage must be fitted securely in the overhead compartment.
Prepare for takeoff, please
Make sure your seat belt is securely fastened.
We remind you that this is a non-smoking flight.
We will be flying at an altitude of…..
We will be flying at a height of 4000m
Please turn off all mobile phones and electronic devices.
The jukebox is there for you to listen to.
Please fasten your belt.
No smoking is allowed during the flight.
Press the button above your seat if you need anything
Please remember to switch off your mobile phone
Please pay attention to this short safety demonstration

Passenger-passenger dialogue (on the plane)
A: Excuse me, I think you are in my seat.
B: Oh, what is your seat number?
A: It is number 60A.
B: You are right, my seat is 60B.
A: Thanks. I'm Ben Jackson.
B: My name is Chris Brown. Nice to meet you, Ben
A: Pleased to meet you too.
B: This is my first flight. Please, could you help and tell me what to do?
A: For sure. Have you switched off your mobile?
B: Yes, I have done that.
A: Now, fasten your seat belt and be ready for take-off.
B: What time are we landing in London?
A: At 10 am. It is a two-hour flight
B: Thanks.

Useful phrases for plane passengers' conversation

Passenger 1
Can we switch seats, please?
What is your seat number?
Where are you from?
Where are you travelling to?
Is this your first flight to London?
Can you help me put this in the overhead compartment?
Excuse me; I think you are in my seat.
What is the flight duration?
What time will we be landing?

Passenger 2

What is your name?
Where are you from?
Nice to meet you.

Serving meals on the plane
A: Excuse me, sir. What would you like to have for dinner?
B: What are the choices?
A: Beef, chicken, or fish.
B: You don't have any vegetarian meals, do you?
A: No, we have none.
B: Okay, I'll take the chicken dish.
A: What would you like to drink?
B: May I know the kinds of soft drinks you have?
A: We have Fanta, Coke, sprite, and Pepsi
B: None of my favourites. I want water, please.
A: Still or sparkling water?
B: Still water.
A: Here you go. Enjoy your meal
B: Thanks a lot.

Useful phrases for flight attendant -passenger conversation
Flight-attendant :
Could you please put that in the overhead locker?
What's your seat number?
Could you fill out this form, please?
Do you care for a drink?
Would you like food or
What would you like to have for dinner?
Do you prefer chicken or beef?
Would you like rice or chips?
Coffee or tea?
With sugar?
Lemon or ice?
Would you like a drink, sir?

Passenger :
What are the choices?
What kind of beverages do you have?
What types of soft drinks have you got?
Do you have vegetarian meals?
Can I have extra salt and pepper?
What time will meals be served?
What do you serve for dinner?

Reporting missing luggage (At the luggage claim office.)
A: Good morning sir. What can I do for you?
B: I have a big problem. I can't find my baggage at the luggage carousel.
A: What time did you arrive?
B: I arrived two hours ago, terminal 10 by British Airways.
A: Can I see your luggage card or receipt?
B: Yes, here you are.
A: Wait a minute; let me check our luggage tracking system.
B: Okay.
A: It seems your baggage is delayed or lost.
B: What can I do now?
A: Please fill out this form; write your luggage number and your address.
B: Done, here you are.
A: We will send it to you if we find it.

Useful phrases used at the airport luggage claim office
Luggage agent :

Where are you coming from?
What flight were you on?
What is your flight number?
Could you give details of your suitcase?
What colour is your suitcase?
What brand is your suitcase?
What was inside it?
What is it made of?
Did you have a tag on your suitcase?
Can you tell me your name, please?
May I see your claim tag?
Can I see your boarding pass and passport?
Were you at the luggage claim area in time?
Did you watch the luggage conveyor belt carefully?

Traveller :
Is this a lost luggage office?
Can I report my missing luggage here?
Can you check your system for this?
Can you check if it is missing or delayed?
Are you sure that it is delayed?
When will it arrive if it is delayed?
When can I get it back?
What will happen if you can't find it?
I didn't see my suitcase on the carousel.

TRAVEL BY ROAD

Booking a taxi

A: Hello. Is that an ABC cab?
B: Yes, how can I help you?
A: It is Peter Johnson. Can you come to pick me up tomorrow morning?
B: Of course I can. At what time?
A: At 6 am.
B: Where do you want me to take you?
A: To the airport?
A: OK. And your address?
B: My address is Brown Street 2/4.
A: Thanks. I will be there.
B: Great. Please, don't be late.
A: For sure I won't. See you tomorrow at six o'clock.
B: See you,

<u>Useful phrases for booking a taxi</u>
<u>Taxi driver:</u>
Where would you like to go?
Where will I drive you to?
Where is your destination?
Where are you going?
How many of you are going?
How many people are travelling?
Do you have a lot of luggage?
How many pieces of luggage do you have?
Do you want a small or a big car?
Would you prefer an AC or a non-AC car?
What time should I come for you?
What time do you want me to be there?
Would you like me to bring you back?

Passenger:
Could you take a taxi to the Hilton Hotel?
Could you take me to the airport?
How long will it take to get there?
Do you use a meter?
How much would that cost?
I would like to book a taxi.
I want to book a cab to the airport.
I want a comfortable and clean car.

Taxi driver and passenger dialogue

A: Good morning. Could you take me to the Bulgarian Embassy?
B: Yes. Do you have the address?
A: Yes, here you go.
B: What time do you have to be there?
A: I have to be there before two o'clock.
B: We have only forty minutes left.
A: Yes. Please take the quickest route without any traffic jams.
B: I will do my best to get there on time. Do you work at the Embassy?
A: No. I am just going for a visa.
B: Here we are. You have to drop off here because of no parking over there.
A: Thank you for driving safely. What is the fare?
B: That's $60
A: Here you go. Please keep the change.

Useful phrases Taxi-driver and passenger conversation

Taxi drivers questions
Where are you going?
Where are you heading to?
Where do I take you to?
Do you have the address of the embassy?
Can I put your bags in the trunk?
Are you in a hurry?
Would you prefer to go there via X or Y?
Which train station are you going to?
Where exactly do you want to drop off?
Which place would you drop off?

It might take 30 minutes to get there.
There is a lot of traffic.
This is the peak hour.

Passenger's questions
Can you take me to the airport?
Can you take the quickest route?
Which is the fastest route to get there?
How much is the fare?
How much is the toll?
Can you come to pick me up at 4 pm?
Could you help me with the bags?

Hiring a car dialogue (at car rental)
A: Good Morning Sir. May I help you?
B: Yes, I want to rent a car.
A: Do you want to hire a full-size, mid-size, or compact, sir?
B: I want an automatic mid-size model with air conditioning.
A: No problem.
B: How much does it cost?
A: It costs £50 a day with unlimited mileage.
B: Does this include collision damage waiver and personal accident insurance?
A: No, you also have to pay £7 per day for a full coverage insurance
B: That's altogether £ 57 per day.
A: Yes. For how many days do you want this car?
B: For two days.
A: Could I see your driving license and credit card, please?
B: Here you are.
A: Please fill out this form and sign.

Useful phrases used at the car rental
Worker's questions
What is your full name?
Under what name should I make the booking?
Do you have an international driving license?
What type of license have you got?
What types of cars would you like?
How long do you need the car?
How would you like to pay?
Have you ever rented a car before?
What is your reason for renting a car?

Traveller's questions
How much would a midsize car cost?
What time do I have to bring it back?
What types of cars do you have?
Can I choose the make and model of the car??

Other expressions
Here are the keys to the car.
Please remember to fill the tank.
Pick your car at the garage.
It needs to come back before 2 pm tomorrow.
Thank you, drive safely.

Car service dialogue
A: Good morning sir. How can I help you?
B: Hi there. I'd like to arrange to have my car serviced.
A: You are at the right place.
B: Is your garage affiliated with any car service code?
A: Of course, we are.
B: **Do you service all types of cars and trucks?**
A: Of course, we do. **What year and model is your car?**
B: It's a two-year-old BMV....
A: Has it been serviced following the manufacturer's schedules before?
B: Yes, it has. The last service was six months ago.
A: What is the problem with your car now?
B: Nothing special, I just want preventive maintenance.
 A: Your car is two years old now, why not book a full service?
B: You are right. When can you bring it here for full service?
A: You can bring it tomorrow.

<u>Useful phrases used at a car service station</u>
<u>Mechanic's questions</u>

What is the problem?
What car parts do you want to change?
Do you want me to replace the brake pads?
Would you like me to run a full diagnostic?
Do you know where the sound is coming from?
Is the sound coming from the engine?
Would you like to get the tires balanced?
When did you service your car last?
When last did you replace this?
How often do you change the brake pads?
Do you have your car manual?

<u>Car owner's questions</u>
Can I get a tune-up?
How often should I change the oil?
Can you repair this today?
When will my car be ready?
I have problems starting my car.
There is a problem with my engine.

Buying petrol dialogue (at the gas station)
A: Good morning. Can I help you?
B: Yes, of course. Can you put 10 litres of petrol for me
A: Which car?
B: That red sports car.
A: OK, Sir. Leaded or unleaded petrol?
B: Unleaded
A: Anything else?
B: Yes, Can you also check the oil level, please?
A: I have put petrol and the oil level is maximum.
B: Thanks. How much do I pay?
A: You have to pay thirty-two dollars.
B: Here you are. Keep the change.
A: Thank you. Safe journey.

Useful phrases used at a fuel station

Fuel buyer's questions

Can you check my wiper fluid?
Can you give me $40 worth of petrol?
Can you do my windows?
Could you wash my windows?
How much is a litre?
How much do I pay?
Twenty dollars worth of petrol, please?
I don't have much gas.
I don't have enough petrol.
I want to fill up my petrol tank.
I run out of gas.
I need to fill up my oil tank.
Here is the key to the tank.

Attendant's questions

Do you want me to fill up your gas tank?
Does your car take gas or petrol?
Do you want me to check the oil also?
Would you like to pump up your tyres?
What grade of gas do you want?
Do you prefer leaded or unleaded petrol?
Check the wiper fluid for you.
Would you like me to check your tire pressure?

Traffic control dialogue
A: Stop the car!
B: Yes, sir
A: Can I see your ID, driving license, and car owner's card?
B: Yes, here they go. Have I violated any traffic rules?
A: You were driving very fast.
B: Sorry. But I didn't exceed the speed limit.
A: Of course, you did. It is 50mph here. Could you blow this breathalyser, sir?
B: Sure.
A: Well, no alcohol. Would you mind opening your boot?
B: It is open. Is everything ok?
A: No, for reckless driving you have to pay a $30 fine.
B: OK here you go. Can I go now?
A: Yes. Here are your documents. Drive safely!

<u>Useful phrases used at a police checkpoint</u>
<u>Traffic police's questions</u>
Are you an owner-driver?
Have you forgotten the traffic rules?
Can I have your driving license?
Can I see your ID and car owner's card?
Where is your car insurance receipt?
Do you have a driving licence?
Please can you show me the RC book?
Can I see the inside of your boot?
Can you switch on your headlights?

<u>Driver's questions</u>
What have I done wrong?
Did I do anything wrong?
Can I see your police ID?
What traffic rules have I violated?
Other expressions
Stop the vehicle! Get down!
I see. You are not an owner-driver.
You exceeded the speed limit.
You are not allowed to park here.
You aren't wearing your seat belt.
You didn't obey the traffic rules.

In a car dialogue
A: John, Be more careful! You nearly hit that young girl at the pedestrian crossing
B: You are right; I didn't see her in time.
A: Please slow down, you are driving too fast.
B: Ok. You know we departed late and I want to get to London on time.
A: I think the most important is to get there safely.
 B: Of course, we will get there safely. I always drive carefully.
A: Well, being careful is one, and keeping the traffic rules is the other.
B: Have I done any other thing wrong?
A: Yes, I see you don't pay attention to road signs and speed limits.
B: Of course I do.
A: No you don't. The town speed limit here is 50 kilometres per hour.
B: And my speed?
A: Your speedometer is showing 120 Km/h.
B: Ok I will be vigilant and keep to traffic rules.

<u>Back seat driver's comments</u>

<u>Backseat driver:</u>

Be more careful!
Can you roll down the window?
Don't go that way!
Stop using the phone while driving.
Mind the speed limit.
No smoking, please
O-M-G! What are you doing?
Put on your seat belt.
Red light! Red light!
Slow down!
You are going too slowly.
You should turn left there.
Speed up! We are late.
Stop the car.
Take a right up there.
What a dirty car! Clean it up.
You are driving too fast.

Hitchhiking (on the highway)
A: Okay, I try to stop this truck.
B: Jump in.
A: Good morning. Thank you for stopping.
B: Where are you heading to?
A: My final destination is Warsaw.
B: You are damn lucky because I'm driving straight to Warsaw.
A: My name is Juszenko.
A: I am Adam. Juszenko, where are you from?
B: I am from Ukraine.
A: What are you doing here in Poland?
B: I am going to look for a job in Warsaw.
A: I wish you good luck.
B: Thank you for giving me a ride
Useful phrases for hitchhiking

Driver's questions

Where are you travelling to?
 Where do you want to go?
Where are you heading to?
How often do you hitchhike?
Do you stop every car?
How long have you been waiting here?
No problem, I am going that way.

Hitchhiker's questions

Good afternoon sir
Can you give me a ride?
Can you give me a lift to the next city?
I am going to…..Is it on your way?
Can you drop me at the next gas station?
Can I get out here?
Thank you for the ride.
Excuse me for stopping you.
I am sorry for disturbing your travel.

Waiting for a bus (at bus stop dialogue)
A: Excuse me, has bus number 18 arrived?
B: I'm afraid it has just passed. I also missed it.
A: Oh, how can me to the airport now? Is there any taxi rank near
here?
B: Sorry, but there is none.
A: Does any other bus go from here to the airport?
B: Yes. Bus number 10 also runs to the airport.
A: How long will it take to get there?
B: It will take only 15 minutes. It is an express bus.
A: Can I buy a ticket on the bus?
B: No. you can't.
A: Is there a nearby place where I can buy a bus ticket?
B: No, there isn't but I can give you one. I am also going to the airport.
A: Thank you. What time is this bus?
B: We are lucky, it is just coming.

Useful phrases used at the bus stop
Traveller's questions
Do you live in this city?
Can I buy a ticket on the bus?
What bus do I take to get to the airport?
Which bus goes to the train station?
What bus takes me to the specialist hospital?
Where do I catch the bus to the airport?
Do long-distance buses also stop here?
Is this bus stop only for local buses?
Does bus number 12 stop here?
How often does bus 18 stop here?
How long will the next bus be?
Where are you heading to?
How many stops is the stadium from here??
Does this bus go toward the….?
Does bus number 10 go to the park?
I want to go to the stadium, which bus goes there?
I want to go to….where do I get off?
My bus is late. Is there a taxi rank near here?

Useful expressions
You need to take bus number 10 or 12.
It is five stops from here.
You can take bus 10 or 12 to get there.

On the bus dialogue (in the wrong bus)
A: Excuse me; do you live in this city?
B: Yes, I do.
A: Am I on the right bus to the Specialist Hospital?
B: Well, this bus turns right at the junction and the hospital is on the left.
A: Is the hospital still far from the junction?
B: Yes, it is about three kilometres
A: Oh, how do I get there?
B: You have to get off at the last bus stop before the junction.
A: What do I do next?
B: Go to the bus stop on the left and take bus 25 or 85.
A: Could you please tell me when to jump off?
B: For sure I will.
A: Thank you.

<u>Useful phrases used on a bus</u>

<u>Passenger's questions</u>
Is this seat free?
Am I on the right bus to….?
May I sit here?
What is the next bus stop?
What is this bus stop?
Could you please tell me where to jump off?
Does this bus go to……..?
Does this bus stop anywhere near…..?
Excuse me, can I ask you something?
How many stops to the post office?
Is the (post office) still far from here?
Where do I get off?

City bus
City bus timetable/ schedule
City bus routes
City bus depot

Asking about the bus timetable

A: How can I help you?
B: What time does the bus from Warsaw to Gdansk arrive here?
A: It arrives at 10 am.
A: Does it normally arrive on time?
B: Yes, it does.
B: What time does it leave?
A: It leaves at ten-fifteen.
B: Can I buy the ticket for this bus here?
A: No, you can only buy it from the bus driver.
B: Why?
A: This is because it is not our bus. It is a private bus.
B: Well, does it usually have vacant seats?
A: Yes, it does. Many people get down here.
B: Thank you for the information

<u>Useful phrases used at the bus station</u>

<u>Passenger's questions</u>
What is the best way to get to the zoo?
What time is the next bus to the market?
What is the arrival time of the bus from London?
What time does the earliest bus to Paris leave?
What time does the last bus from Paris arrive?
How long does the journey take?
Does the 8:30 bus to Gdansk stop at the Eastern bus station?
What type of bus is that?
Is it a fast bus or an express bus?
How often do buses run to…?
Which bus stand is the bus to the train station?
Can I buy the ticket for this bus here?
Can I buy the ticket for this bus?
Can I book the ticket online?
Can I buy the ticket in advance?
Which counter can I buy the ticket?
Where is the ticket office?
Where is the ticket machine?
Where are you going?
Does an express bus go to the stadium?

TRAVELLING BY RAIL

Asking about the train (At the train inquiry office)

A: Good Morning. How can I help you?
B: Good morning. What time is the next train to London?
A: It is at 11.30
B: Is it a slow or fast train?
A: It is a fast and direct train
B: Which platform does it go from?
A: From platform 2
B: What time will it arrive in London?
A: The arrival time there is 14:30.
B: That's great because I have to be there before 4 pm.
A: Anything else?
B: Yes. Please could you tell me where the waiting room is?
A: Go straight; it is there on the left.
B: Thank you. Goodbye

Useful phrases used at the train inquiry office
<u>Passenger's questions:</u>
Can you give me information about trains to…?
When does the overnight train from Paris get in?
What time does the train from Gdansk arrive?
What is the arrival time of the train from Paris?
What is the departure time of the train to Benin?
What time does the train to Paris leave?
Is there another train to London today?
What platform does the train leave from?
How long does it take to get to London?
Is it a direct train or do I have to change?
Is there any connection by train to…?
Where am I supposed to transfer?
How often do trains run to Warsaw?
What time is the next train to Warsaw?
What time is the last train to Warsaw?
What type of train is that?
Is this a fast train?
Do I have to change the train?

Buying a train ticket

A: Good morning sir. Can I help you?
B: Yes. Can I have a train ticket to Gdansk, please?
A: Trains to Gdansk are at 11 am and 1 pm. For which one?
B: Are they express or slow trains?
A: Only the one at one o'clock is an express train.
B: I see. I want a ticket for the one o'clock train
A: What type of ticket do you want?
B: A first-class reserved seat ticket.
A: Single or return?
B: Single.
A: In smoking or non-smoking compartment?
B: Non-smoker.
A: Here's your ticket and that's $ 40.
B: Here you go. Thank you.

Useful phrases used at the train ticket office

Ticket clerk :
Single or return ticket?
Smoking or non-smoking compartment?
When are you coming back??
When will you be coming back?
When would you like to return?
When would you like to travel?
Which berth do you prefer lower or upper?
Which train would you like to take?
Do you want a senior citizen's single?
Do you want a first-class single?
Do you want a child return ticket?
Do you want a first-class return?

Traveller :
A single ticket to London, please?
A return ticket to London, please?
Can I book a berth on the sleeper to….?
Can I buy the return ticket now as well?
Can I get a student discount?
Can I have a reserved seat ticket, please?
Can I reserve a seat on the train to Warsaw?
How much is a first-class single to Warsaw?
How much is a single to Benin?
Are there any reductions for off-peak travel?

Talking about a delayed train.
A: Excuse me, Madam. This is platform 4, isn't it?
B: Yes, it is.
A: I am late. My train was supposed to be here 10 minutes ago.
B: Which Train?
A: Ten o'clock train to Poznan.
B: You are lucky. This train is delayed by 40 minutes.
A: Thank God. Are you also waiting for this train?
B: Yes and I am also travelling to Poznan.
A: I have to be in Poznan by 2 pm and I can only make it with this train.
B: I hope we will be in Poznan before two.
A: By the way, my name is Adam
B: Adam, nice to meet you. I am Alice
A: Alice, nice to meet you too.

<u>Useful phrases used on the platform</u>

<u>Traveller :</u>
Can I buy a ticket on the train?
Where is the platform number 10?
Is this the right platform for London?
Which platform do I need for Gdansk?
Where can I get information about the train delay?
Where can I check the train timetable?
How much luggage can I carry on the train?

<u>Train platform announcements:</u>
Attention passengers, the train to Warsaw is now approaching platform 4.
Attention passengers the train from (Paris) is arriving at platform five.
The next train to arrive at platform 2 is the7.30 from (Warsaw)
The next train to depart from platform 2 will be the7.30 to (Berlin)
Attention passengers, this platform terminates here. Please make your way to platform 4
Attention passengers, we are being delayed due to…….
Attention passengers for the 7.30 train to Warsaw, this train is delayed by 30 minutes

On train dialogue
A: Excuse me, is this seat free?
B: Yes, it is.
A: Hi, do you speak English?
B: Yes, I do.
A: I'm Peter Jackson. I'm English
B: Hi Peter. My name's Eve Tusk. I'm Polish.
A: Nice to meet you, Eve.
B: Nice to meet you too, Peter. Is this your first visit to Poland?
A: Yes and this is my first train trip here in Poland.
B: Where are you traveling to?
A: I'm travelling to Poznan. And your destination?
B: I'm travelling to Wroclaw. What other Polish cities do you plan to visit?
A: I plan to visit Cracow and then travel to Gdansk and Masuria region.
B: Good plan. I wish you a nice stay.

Useful phrases used on the train

Traveller :
Does this train stop at….?
Could you tell me when we get to….?
Excuse me. Is this seat taken?
 Is this seat free?
Do you mind if I sit here?
Is there a buffet car on this train?
Do you mind if I open the window?
What time do we arrive in….?
What's the next train stop?
How many more stops are there before we get to….?
This seat is occupied
Excuse me; I think this is my seat.

Train conductor :
Can you show me your ticket?
Isn't this ticket for second class?
We are now approaching….
This train terminates here.

Luggage storage dialogue (At the train station)
A: Welcome, Sir. How can I help you?
B: Can I store my baggage here?
A: Yes. How many pieces of baggage do you have?
B: I have two big travel bags and a small suitcase.
A: Do you want to store them in our storeroom or lockers?
B: In your storeroom. What is the maximum storing time?
A: It is 72 hours.
B: What is the storage price?
A: It is $10 per bag/day.
B: That's ok.
A: Please fill out and sign this form. Are there any breakable items in the bags?
B: Here is the signed form. I don't have anything breakable.
A: That's all. Here is your receipt.

Useful phrases used at the train station luggage
Luggage room worker :

Do you want to store your bags in our storeroom or lockers?
Does your bag contain any breakables?
How many pieces of baggage do you have?
How long do you plan to keep your luggage here?
What time will you pick up your baggage?
You have to pay $6 per day.
Storage in lockers is $3 for a small bag and $4 for a big bag.

Traveller :
Do you offer both short and long-term storage?
Can I store my baggage here?
Do you still have storage space here?
What is the maximum storing time?
How much do I pay?

Lost and found office dialogue (At the train station)
A: Hello. What is the problem?
B: I lost my wallet here yesterday. I noticed this when I got home.
A: Did you lose it on a train or here at the train station?
B: At the station. I wasn't on a train; I only escorted my friend here.
A: What does your wallet look like?
B: It is a big rectangular brown wallet with cardholders and a pocket for banknotes
A: What does it contain?
B: It contains my ID card, business cards, and my picture.
A: Two wallets match your description. Which one is yours?
B: The one on the left.
A: OK. Let me check its content. Yes, your photo and ID card are here.
B: Thank you a lot.
A: Please sign here and take your wallet.

<u>Useful phrases used at lost and found office</u>

What did you lose?
What type of bag did you lose?
What does your bag look like?
What is your bag size?
What is the shape of your bag?
How big is it?
What colour is it?
Are there any labels or pictures on your bag?
What is it made of?
What does it contain?
Where did you leave it?
Did you lose it in the station or on the train?
When last did you have it?
When was the last time you saw it?
Which day was that?
Can you describe it?
Can you fill this form with your data?
Could you describe your bag in this form?

TRAVEL BY SEA

Asking about cruises

A: Hello, can I be of any help?
B: What cruises do you have in June?
A: We have two cruises: the Caribbean, and the Baltic cruise.
B: Who is the tour operator of the Baltic cruise
A: The tour operator is MSC Cruises
B: What type of ship is that?
A: It is an MSC Preziosa.
B: Where is the ship departing from?
A: From Hamburg
B: How many countries will the Passengers visit?
A: Five countries: Germany, Sweden, Finland, Russia, and Poland.
B: What is the cruise duration (trip length)?
A: That will be 12 nights.
B: Thank you for the information.

Useful phrases used at the cruise ship agency
Cruise agent :
What time of the year do you want to travel?
Which cruise vacation are you interested in?
What cruise line is your preference?
Are you travelling alone?
Would you like adjoining cabins for families?

Traveller :
What type of vessel is the cruise ship?
How many days of cruise is that?
What are the cabins like?
What is the cruise fare?
How long will the cruise trip last?
Do you organize a tour at each port?
Is this a cruise ship or a gigantic mega-liner?
Do you give a discount for group travel?
How much time will we spend at each port?
What types of official ID do I need to have?
How many ports will the ship call at?
How many times will passengers go ashore?
Do you organize transportation to and from the departure port?
What entertainment and activities does the ship offer?

Booking a cabin (At the cruise ship agency)
A: Good day sir. How can I help you?
B: I would like to book a cabin on the next cruise ship to the Caribbean.
A: The next Caribbean cruise is on June 22nd; is this ok for you?
B: Well, what is the cruise duration?
A: This is 21 nights.
B: Which major cities will the cruise ship dock?
A: It will dock at Southampton and New York.
B: Ok. What is the fare?
A: Do you want an inside cabin, outside, or balcony cabin?
B: I want an inside cabin.
A: Do you prefer a cabin on the lower or upper deck?
B: I prefer a lower deck cabin.
A: The price is $1777 per person
B: Here's my passport, please book me on this.

Useful phrases for booking a cabin
Cruise agent:
What cabin location would you like?
What type of cabin do you want?
Do you want :
Cabin at the front or back of the ship?
Inside or ocean view cabin?
First-class or second-class cabin?
Single or double occupancy?

Traveller :
Can I book a cabin on the next cruise?
Are fares by a person or by cabin?

Expressions
Cruise liner/ship
Disney cruise line
Carnival cruise line
Caribbean cruise line
Norwegian cruise line
Premium cruise line
Celebrity cruise line
World cruise

Talking about cruise holidays (Last holiday cruise)
A: John, where did you spend your holidays?
B: I spent my holidays joyfully on a ship?
A: On a ship?
B: Yes, I went on a holiday cruise.
A: Great. Did you go on the world, Caribbean, or Mediterranean cruise?
B: I went on a Caribbean cruise.
A: How was it?
B: It was a smooth voyage, full of excitement and entertainment.
A: Where did you start your holiday cruise?
B: From Hamburg
A: How many ports did your cruise ship call?
B: At seven ports
A: Did you go ashore?
B: Of course, we did. Three times.

Useful phrases to talk about cruise holidays
Have you ever gone on a holiday cruise?
Did you take the cruise with friends?
Who went on a holiday cruise with you?
How was your holiday cruise?
Where did you sail from?
Did you go ashore during the cruise?
Did you share a cabin with someone?
Which ports did you call?
Which countries did you go ashore?
Which famous people were on the cruise?

Where are you going on a cruise this summer?
What do you think of a booze cruise?
Did you experience problems during the voyage?

It is $90 per person per day.
We had a very smooth voyage
We went on a cruise to Norwegian Fjord.
I shared a cabin with a Polish friend.
The views of the coastlines were fantastic
I was seasick at the beginning.

Buying a ferry ticket (At the seaport)
A: Good morning. How can I help you?
B: Good morning. What time is the next ferry to the Island?
A: The next ferry is at 10:30 a.m.
B: Can I still get a place on this ferry?
A: It depends. Are you travelling with someone?
B: Alone
A: I have two spaces in a four-berth cabin. Can this be?
B: Yes of course
A: Would you prefer the lower or the upper berth?
B: Upper berth. What is the ferry fare?
A: Do you want a single or return ticket?
B: A return ticket.
A: That's $50.
B: Here it is. Thanks and Goodbye.

Useful phrases for buying a ferry ticket

Ferry Ticket clerk:

What type of cabin do you want?
Do you want a four-berth or two-berth cabin?
Do you prefer the lower or the upper berth?
Would you like to book now?

Traveller :
Are there any morning proms to…?
Can I get a place on the ferry to the Island?
When is the next ferry to Dover due?
When does the next ferry leave?
What is the sailing duration?
How much is the ticket?
What is the ferry fare?
Are there any discounts for a return ticket?

TOURISM and TRAVELLERS
Applying for a passport (At passport office)

A: Please be seated. How can I help you?
B: Good morning. I want to get a passport.
A: Have you filled out the passport application form?
B: Yes, here you are.
A: Can I have copies of your birth certificate and ID card?
B: Yes, here they go.
A: May I see the originals of these?
B: Yes, of course.
A: Please put your fingerprint here and sign your signature.
B: Anything else?
A: Yes, your two passport photos and the passport fee payment receipt.
B: Done. This is the receipt.
A: That's all. Come here to collect your passport in two weeks.

Useful phrases used at the passport office
Passport applicant's questions

Excuse me; can I apply for a passport here?
Can I have a passport application form?
Can I apply for a passport online?
What documents are needed?
What things are required?
Do I have to pay?
How much is the passport fee?
How many passport photos must I submit?
What do I do with this application?
Where do I submit the application form?
How long will it take to process this?
When will my passport be ready?

Passport officer's questions

Are you applying for a passport for the first time?
 Have you filled out the application form?

Getting a visa (Visa interview dialogue)
A: Please have a seat. May I know your full name?
B: Michael Edwin Mugabe.
A: Have you been to the US before?
B: Yes. I was there on vacation three years ago.
A: What type of Visa have you applied for this time?
B: I have applied for a student visa.
A: What and where do you wish to study in the US?
B: I have got an admission to study Computer Science at Harvard University.
A: Who is going to pay your tuition fees and other costs?
B: Our federal Ministry of Education. I have got a scholarship.
A: That's all. You will get a call from us soon.
B: Thank you for your time

Useful phrases used at the visa interview
Visa officer :
What is your full name?
May I know your name?
Tell me about yourself
What is your purpose in going to the USA??
Have you got a valid passport?
What country issued your passport?
What type of visa have you applied for?
When did you submit your visa application?
What university are you going to study?
Can I see your original birth certificate?
What do you plan to do after your studies?
Who is going to pay your tuition fees and living costs?

Are you travelling with someone
Can you show me your passport?
Does your family live in the USA?
Have you been to the US before?
Do you like American food?
What do you do for fun?
What are you going to study?
Why do you wish to study in the US?

Visa applicant :

How long am I authorized to stay? I applied for a Student Visa

Arranging holidays (At travel agency)
A: Good morning. Can I help you?
B: I hope so. I want to get some information.
A: What do you want to know?
B: What are the most popular holiday destinations this summer?
A: The most popular holiday destinations are Greece, Spain, and Egypt.
B: What Greek tour packages do you have?
A: At the moment we have a Mykonos tour and a sightseeing tour of Los Island.
B: When is the next tour to Los Island?
A: It starts on Wednesday the 20th.
B: What is the duration of this tour?
A: It is a 7-day tour.
B: What is the price?
A: It is $1500
B: Thank you for the information.

Useful phrases used at the travel agency
Travel agent :
What is your holiday destination?
What city do you intend to travel to?
When do you want to go?
Do you want to travel by road, air, or sea?
What type of ticket would you like?
Do you wish to buy a bus or a plane ticket?
What airline do you prefer?
How many people are for group travel?
Which airport do you want to leave?
How many people are travelling?
What type of hotel do you want to stay in?
One way or round trip?

Traveller :
What vacation packages do you have?
Do you have any last-minute package holiday deals?
Could you book me a place on a cruise ship to Lagos?
What does the holiday package include?
How much is a two-week holiday in Egypt?
What tropical country do you propose?
Do you organize group travels to Safari?
Is there any special hunting or fishing trip?
Where is the best holiday resort in Bulgaria?
What is the best air connection to Sydney?
Are the emergency services in this brochure?
What emergency services should I call if needed?
Could I get some information about your cruises?
Have you got any attractive offers for summer?

Travel problems (a ten-hour layover)
A: John, did you have a direct flight from Poland to Nigeria?
B: No, I had a ten-hour layover in Sofia.
A: Ten hours?
B: Yes, we landed in Sofia at noon and I had my flight at 10 pm.
A: What did you do during this time?
B: We stayed, rested, and had dinner at the airport hotel.
A: Is the airport hotel on the airport premises?
B: No, it isn't. But there is a shuttle bus service to the hotel.
A: Did you visit the city of Sofia?
B: No, I didn't because I was tired.
A: Did you pay for the hotel?
B: The airline paid for this. It was included in the fare.
A: What a long nice flight!

<u>Useful phrases to talk about travel problems</u>

Have you ever missed your flight?
Have you ever had your flight cancelled?
Have you ever had your flight delayed?
Have you ever had your luggage missed?
Have you ever had your luggage left behind or delayed?
Have you ever had your luggage damaged on the plane?
Have you ever had your wallet stolen at the airport?
Have you ever had to pay unexpected luggage fees?
Have you ever hadn't got money for excess luggage?
Have you ever been sick in a foreign country without any insurance?
Have you ever forgotten your travel documents at home?
Have you ever felt very lonely during travel?
Have you ever lost your phone?
Have you ever had a problem with customs control?
Have you ever forgotten your travel documents?
Have you ever had a problem with getting a visa?
Have you ever had flight altitude sickness?
Have you ever had airplane ear problems?
left flight ticket at home?
Have you ever faced language barriers?
Have you ever run out of money during travel?

Cashing travellers' cheques (At the bank)
A: Good afternoon, sir. Can I be of any assistance?
B: Yes, I would like to cash my traveller's cheque.
A: How much do you want to cash?
B: I want to change the $500 cheque.
A: Do you want this in dollars or local currency?
B: In local currency.
A: Can I see your passport or ID card?
B: Yes, here's my passport.
A: Okay. Please countersign the cheque here.
B: Sure, with today's date.
A: Here is your money.
B: Thank you a lot. Goodbye.

Useful phrases for cashing a cheque

Bank cashier
What can I help you with?
What type of cheque do you want to cash?
What types of cheques do you have?
What currency are the cheques?
What currency do you want?
Can I have your photo ID?
Could you complete this form, please?
Could you countersign here, please?
How much do you want to cash?
Let me check the cheques' serial numbers

Traveller
Can I cash traveller's cheques here?
Do you accept traveller's cheques here?
Are these traveller's cheques still valid?
Are there any charges for this?
What is the cash-in fee?
What is the exchange rate for the Euro?

Getting information about a hotel

A: AB Airport Hotel. How can I help you?

B: I am calling from the airport. Can I get some information about your hotel?

A: What do you want to know?

B: What is the star rating of your hotel?

A: It is a five-star hotel.

B: Is your hotel on the airport premises?

A: No, but it is not far from the airport.

B: Great. How far is your hotel from the airport?

A: It's about six kilometres

B: Do you provide airport shuttle service?

A: Yes, of course. We provide a free airport shuttle service.

B: Do you have any vacant rooms?

A: Yes, we have free single rooms.

B: Thank you for the information

A: My pleasure.

Useful phrases to ask about hotels

Traveller

Where is your hotel situated?

What type of hotel is it?

How far is your hotel from the airport?

Do you provide an airport shuttle service?

How often do shuttle buses run to the airport?

Is your hotel name written on the buses?

Where can I catch the shuttle bus at the airport?

What facilities does your hotel have?

Do you charge guests by the hour or daily?

What is your rate per night for a room?

How much is your room rate per night?

What is the price for a double room?

What is the price per night?

What are the payment options?

How much is your daily charge?

Booking a hotel room (abort airport hotel)
A: AB Airport Hotel. How can I help you?
B: I want to book a room. Do you have a vacancy?
A: Single or double room?
B: A single room for a night. I have a flight at 8 am tomorrow.
A: Yes, we have.
B: Great. Do you charge guests by the hour?
A: No, only per night.
B: What is your checking-in time?
A: The check-in time is 9 am.
B: What is the rate?
A: For a single room, it is $100 per night
B: My name is Adam Brown. I will be there at your hotel soon.
A: Ok we are waiting for you.

Useful phrases for booking a hotel room
Traveller:

Do you have any vacancies?
Are there any vacant rooms here?
Have you any vacant rooms?
Have you got a double room free?
Have you got any rooms available?
Do you have any single room left?
Is it a back or front room?
Can I reserve a room for…..?
Can I book two rooms for…?
Could I have a double room?
How much is the charge per night?
How much is your room rate per night?
What is the price for a double room?
What is the price per night?
What are the payment options?

Hotel receptionist :
Hotel Hilton, how can help you?
Would you like to make a reservation now?
Would you like to book a room for Monday?
What sort of room would you like?
What kind of room do you need?
Would you like a single or double room?
A room with a bath or with a shower?
How long will you be staying?
How long are you going to stay?
How long will you stay with us?
When is the booking for?
Who is the booking for?
For how many people?
For how many nights?

Checking in at a hotel (At the airport hotel)

A: Good evening sir. How can I help you?
B: My name is Adam Brown. I phoned you from the airport an hour ago.
A: I remember your name. You asked for a single room.
B: Yes, I want a single for the night.
A: Okay, can I have your photo ID?
B: Yes, of course. Here is my passport.
A: All right. Your room is nr 102 and here is your key.
B: Madam, on which floor is this?
A: That is on the first floor and the lift is over there.
B: To what time is your restaurant open??
A: It is open till midnight.
B: Thank you for your help.
A: You are welcome

<u>Useful phrases for checking in at hotels</u>
<u>Hotel receptionist:</u>
Good morning, welcome to AB Hotel.
Can you be of any assistance?
Have you reserved/ booked a room?
When did you make the reservation?
How did you make the booking?
Did you make a reservation directly to us?
Did you confirm your reservation?
When did you confirm your reservation?
Can I have your Reservation slip/number?
Could you sign the register, please?
Have you filled in the registration form?
Has the valet already taken your car?

<u>Hotel guest</u> :
Which floor is the room?
Where is the lift?
What time is breakfast?
Where is breakfast served?
Do I pay now or at checking out?
Could the bellboy help to bring up my suitcase?
What is the check-out time?
What time should I vacate the room?

<u>Useful expressions</u>
I have a reservation for a single room for five days.
 It was booked through my travel agent.
It was a telephone reservation.
I made the booking on the 15th of June.

Requesting a wake-up call (at the airport hotel)
A: Sir, how was your supper?
B: Very delicious dishes in your restaurant.
A: Thank you for your compliment.
B: Could I have my key, room 102?
A: Sure, here you are.
B: Please, what time is the first shuttle bus to the airport in the morning?
A: It is at six O'clock.
B: I have my flight at 8 am. Could you make a wake-up call for me in the morning?
A: Yes. At what time?
B: At five o'clock
A: Room 1-0-2, at five o'clock. Right?
A: Yes, thank you. Good night
B: Sleep well, sir.

<u>Useful phrases for making hotel requests</u>

I would like to order breakfast in room 222, please.
May I have dinner in my room, please?
Can someone bring some coffee to my room, please?
Do you have a valet parking service?
Can your valet parking attendant (valet) park my car underground?
Can you send an extra pillow and blanket, please?
Could you give me a call tomorrow at 8 am?
Could I have a wake-up call tomorrow at 8 am?
Can you send someone to pick up the laundry from my room, please?
Can I have an iron, please?
Could I ask you to extend my stay, please?
Would it be possible to extend my stay to Friday?
Would it be possible for you to send a technician to check my heater?
Could I trouble you to change my room, this one is very noisy?
Could I leave my luggage in your storeroom, please?
Do you mind if I take some guests into my room?
I was wondering if you could give me the city map.?
May I request some swimming pool towels?

Hotel checking out (at the airport hotel)
A: Good morning sir.
B: Good morning. Thank you for the wake-up call.
A: You are welcome.
B: I'd like to check out. Can I have my bill, please?
A: Yes, of course, Mr Brown.
B: How much do I pay?
A: It's altogether $100
B: What are your payment options?
A: You can pay by credit card or in cash.
B: I pay cash.
A: Thank sir. Here is your receipt.
B: Thanks. I enjoyed my one-night stay here.
A: Glad to hear this. Have a nice flight. Goodbye

Useful phrases for hotel checking out
Hotel guest's questions

I want to check it out. Can I have my bill?
Can you tell me what this charge is for?
Can I leave my bags in your storeroom?
What is included in the bill?
What is your checkout time?
What time am I supposed to vacate the room?
What happens if I miss the check-out time?
Does your hotel offer a late checkout?
Can I have a late check-out?
Are there any charges for a late check-out?
Could you call me a taxi, please?
Are there shuttle buses to the airport?
What time is the next shuttle to the airport
Can you send somebody for our bags?

Hotel receptionist's questions
Do you want to check out now?
Are you ready to check out?
Could I have your room number, please?
What room are you checking out of?
May I know your room number, please?
How would you like to pay?
Will you be putting this on your credit card?
How was your stay?
Are you satisfied with your stay here?
Do you need any help with your baggage?
Would you like me to call a taxi for you?
Let me check your room, can you wait, please?
You have to pay a late check-out fee.

Asking for direction (in a new city)
A: Excuse me, where is the nearest bank?
B: What type of bank?
A: A commercial bank.
B: There is one at Brown Street.
A: How far is it from here?
B: It is more than 5 kilometres.
A: That's far. How can I get there then?
B: You can go there by taxi, bus, or by tram.
A: Where is the nearest bus or tram stop?
B: The bus stop is just over there.
A: Which bus do I take?
B: Buses 22 and 108 go there.
A: Thank you. Goodbye

Useful phrases for asking and giving directions

<u>Traveller's questions</u>
 Could you give me some directions, please?
Can you give me directions to the bus stop?
What is the best way of getting to the bus station?
What is the easiest way to get to the post office?
Where is the train station from here?
Could you tell me where it is situated?
Could you tell me where the nearest bank is?
Do you know where the closest bank is?
Can you show me on this map the way to..?
Could you tell me the way to…?
How far is the Polish Embassy from here?
 Could you please tell me where the bus stop is?
Is there a post office this way?

<u>Useful expressions</u>
Go straight ahead /on until you come to…
Go past the post office and then turn right.
Just follow this road until you get to….
Follow the road round to the left
Take the first/second turn on your left.
Stay on this road for five kilometres.
There is a bank across the street near the…..
It is on the right of the supermarket.
It is next to the chemist's
It is opposite the bus station.

Asking about accommodation (**at the tourist information centre**)
A: Welcome to our city, how can I help you?
B: This first time in this city, I'm looking for a place to stay.
A: What type of accommodation do you have in mind?
B: A good hotel. How many hotels are there in this city?
A: There are five hotels, two motels, and a youth hostel.
B: Which hotel is the nearest to the airport?
A: I think the Queen's Hotel is the nearest.
B: What type of hotel is that?
A: It is a five-star hotel.
B: Could you help me to ring this hotel?
A: Yes. Do you want me to book a room or get some information for you?
B: I want to know if they have a vacant single room.

<u>Useful phrases for asking a place to stay</u>

<u>Tourist's information officer's questions:</u>
Welcome to our city, how can I help you?
Do you want a B&B or a hotel?
What type of hotel do you have in mind?
Can I help you to book a room?
<u>Tourist's questions</u>
Can I buy a map of the city here?
Could you help me to ring this hotel?
Do you have a list of hotels, motels, and hostels?
How many hotels are in this city?
Is there a campsite in this city?
What does the hotel provide?
What makes the hotel unique?
Which hotel has good facilities for the disabled?
Which hotel has the best sports facilities?
Which hotel is in the city centre?
Which hotel is the nearest to the airport?
<u>Useful expressions</u>

I can help you to ring some places.
ABC Hotel is a five-star hotel.
King Hotel is a family hotel.
Queen Hotel is a luxury hotel.
I recommend ABC Hotel to you.
ABC Hotel is located/situated near

Asking about places to visit (at the tourist information centre)
A: Good afternoon sir. Do you need some information?
B: Yes. Are there any companies offering a day tour of this city?
A: Unfortunately there is none.
B: Can I buy any brochures or maps of the city here?
A: We have only the maps left.
B: Can I have one?
A: Yes. That's two dollars
B: Here you are. What is the most interesting part of this city?
A: I think that the most interesting part for tourists is our old town.
B: What is the must-see site in this city?
A: The must-see site is our historical museum.
B: Where should I start my sightseeing tour?
A: I propose that you go first to our king's castle.
B: Thank you.

<u>Useful phrases for asking a place to visit</u>
<u>Tourists' / traveller's questions</u>

Which places and sites are worth visiting here?
Is there a place to feast your eyes on gorgeous views?
Do you have a map showing all the must-see sites?
Do you have a brochure on local places of interest?
Do you have lists of the companies offering day tours?
Which is the most interesting part of this city?
What do you recommend that we see?
Where should we start our sightseeing?
Where is the best place to buy souvenirs.?
Can you show me on this map where the best cafe is?

<u>Useful expression</u>
We need some sightseeing advice.
You must visit the castles in the neighbouring city.
There are many historic sites and cathedrals.
I'd suggest seeing our castles, cathedral, and museums.
Don't miss seeing our botanical garden and zoo.
I'm looking for information about the art gallery.

Asking about places to eat (at the tourist information centre)
A: How do you do? How can we help you?
B: We are looking for a good place to eat. Which restaurant do you recommend?
A: I recommend Ben's restaurant to you.
B: What kind of food does the restaurant serve?
A: It serves both local and foreign cuisines.
B: Is it far from here?
A: No, it is within walking distance.
B: Are there any other reasons why we should go there?
A: Yes, there are.
B: What reasons?
A: Their food is very delicious and their waiters are very friendly.
B: Thanks. We'll go there. Please could you give us the address?
A: Sure, here you are.

<u>Useful phrases for asking a place to eat</u>
<u>Information officer's questions</u> /

What kind of food are you thinking about?
Restaurant serving local cuisine?
Are you keen on trying our local food?
There are a lot of good restaurants in this city.
There are a lot of Chinese restaurants here.
You can meet a lot of tourists in…….restaurant.
Their waiters are very nice and friendly
The waiters there speak good English.
There is a good Mexican restaurant there.
I'd recommend AB restaurant to you.
The quality of food there is of the first class.
AB restaurant serves food from different countries.
AB restaurant offers a wide range of specialties.
Ben Restaurant specializes in Vietnamese cuisine.

<u>Traveller's questions</u>

We are looking for a place to eat, can you help us?
Where can we find a vegetarian restaurant?
Are there any restaurants nearby that serve American dishes?
Could you recommend a good nearby place to eat?
Where can we eat delicious local food?
Are there any foreign restaurants in this city?
What kind of food does that restaurant serve?
What kind of restaurant is that?

Asking about events (at the tourist information centre)
A: Hello, what can we do for you?
B: We want to know which events are on in this city this week.
A: Oh, are you new in this city?
B: Yes, we have just arrived.
A: Welcome to our city. There are a series of cultural and sporting events.
B: Great. What events are on here tonight?
A: You will find all the forthcoming events in this pamphlet.
B: How much is this?
A: This is for you. A gift from our city.
B: Thanks. Can we buy any event tickets here?
A: Yes, we still have tickets for a horror film at the Eden cinema tonight.
B: Can I have two tickets?
A: Yes, here you go. That is $20.
B: Thank you a lot for the information

Useful phrases for asking about events
Traveller's questions.
What is the best place to spend the evenings here?
Could you give me information about cultural events?
Do you have information about what things to do here?
Are there any sporting events in the city today?
How many theatres are there in this town?
Which theatre do you recommend?
What's on at the theatre today?
Do you have last-minute tickets to the theatre?
Can we buy a discounted ticket?
Where can we go dancing?
 How many museums do you have in this city?
When do the museums open and close?
Are Museums open on Sundays here?
What date is U2 having their concert here?

Useful expressions
There are only two cinemas in our town.
There is a great horror film at the King cinema.
There are a series of cultural events here this week.
Those leaflets over there are all free.
All forthcoming events are listed in this pamphlet.
You can buy a map and guidebook of the city here
Our city has something for everyone
Our theatres offer a marvelous range of live entertainment
You can find entertainment of all kinds in this city

Talking about holiday plans
A: Have you got any plans for the long vacation?
B: Yes, I have already got two plans.
A: Two plans! What are your plans?
B: My first plan is to go on a tour of England.
A: Great. What cities are you going to visit?
B: I plan to go to London, Manchester, Bristol, and Cambridge
A: For sure this will help you to improve your English.
B: You are joking. My English is perfect. I just want to see what life is like in England
A: What is your second holiday plan?
B: I am going on a package holiday with our family in August.
A: Where to?
B: To Greece. We spent most of our vacations there.
A: I am jealous of you.
B: What about your vacation plans?
A: Unfortunately, I will spend my vacation in our country this year.

<u>Useful phrases for talking about holiday plans.</u>

When will your next vacation start?
What are your holiday plans?
Where are you travelling to?
Where will you spend your holiday?
What countries would you like to visit?
When are you travelling?
How are you going to get there?
Have you booked your vacation?
Who is travelling with you?
Do you want to travel with us?

What are you going to do?
Do you intend to do any vacation jobs?
Are you going on a package holiday?
How are you going to spend your vacation?
Are you planning to spend your vacation abroad?
Do you plan to book your vacation through a travel agency?

Greetings from holidays(On holidays)

A: Hi John, greetings from Gdansk
B: Why from Gdansk?
A: I am here on holiday with my girlfriend.
B: Great, where are you staying?
 A: We are staying at my uncle's house. Now we are at the beach.
B: What is the weather like there and what are you doing?
A: It is sunny and hot, so we are sunbathing, swimming, and sailing.
 B: Gdansk is a beautiful historic town, what have you visited?
A: We have already visited Westerplatte and tomorrow we are going to the zoo.
B: How long are you going to be there?
A: Perhaps, for five days.
B: So you will be back on Friday.
 A: It is possible. I am looking forward to meeting you.
B: Ok. Thanks for calling.

<u>Useful Phrases for talking about ongoing holiday</u>

You are on a beach holiday, aren't you?
Are you with your friends or family?
What hotel are you staying at?
How are you enjoying your holidays?
What is the weather like there?
Is it sunny and hot?
Where are you now?
What are you doing at the moment?
What places have you visited?
Have you tasted any local cuisines?
What local food have you eaten?
What interesting and historic sites have you visited?/

Are there a lot of holidaymakers there?

Last summer holidays (talking about last holidays)
A: Hello John.
B: Hi Peter. What a surprise! When did you return?
A: I came back yesterday evening.
B: How was your vacation?
A: It was a great tour of European countries.
B: What countries did you travel to?
A: I traveled to Bulgaria, Italy, and Greece.
B: Woo! These countries are excellent summer holiday destinations.
How was the weather?
A: The weather was fantastic all the time.
B: Which cities did you visit in Bulgaria?
A: I spent three days in Sofia and a week in Burgas.
B: Burgas is an ideal place for a beach holiday. I was there last year.
A: I took a lot of pictures there, on the splendid Black Sea coast.
B: I'd love to see all the pictures when I visit you tomorrow.

Useful phrases for talking about last holidays

What was your last holiday destination?
When did you travel?
How did you get there?
Did you have any problems during your travel?
Did you have a good time?
What did you do during the day?
What did you do at night?
What cultural events did you attend?
What local souvenirs did you buy?
Were you at museums and theatres?
What holiday activities did you enjoy the most?
Did you take many pictures?
Did you meet many people from other countries?
Did you make new friends?
When did you come back?

TRANSPORTATION and TRAVEL VOCABULARY

Types of trips and travellers
Type of Trips (travels)
A package tour
Tour
Excursion
Trip
Expedition
Voyage
Pilgrimage
Flight
Cruise
Crossing
Weekend break
Stopover
Flying visit
Extended stay

Types of Travellers
Budget travellers
Adventure travellers
Cultural travellers
Luxury travellers
Family travellers
Solo travellers
Nature lovers
Wellness travellers
Volunteer traveller
Business travellers
Education traveller
Road enthusiasts
Rail enthusiasts
Photography enthusiasts
Culture enthusiasts
Foodie
History buffs

Travelers
Cyclist
Motorcyclist
Chauffeur
Taxi driver
Automobilist
Motorist
Trunk drivers
backpackers
Pilots
Sailors
Seafarers
Peddler
Commuter
Passengers
Pedestrian
Sightseers
Holidaymakers
Excursionist
Tourists
Explorers
Adventurer
Itinerant
Transmigrante
Immigrants
Refugees
Hitchhiker
Hiker
Trekker
Pilgrims
Hadji
Nomad

Air transport-related terms
Airlines
Airline headquarters
Airline offices
Flight training schools
Air navigation service providers
air ticket/plane ticket/flight ticket
one –way ticket
open ticket
ok ticket
gate number
airline/airway/air lane
baggage /luggage
hand baggage
excess baggage
excess luggage cost
lost baggage
suitcase
briefcase
carry-on bag
check-in counter
reporting time
check-in time
departure time
arrival time
connecting time
date of return
date of arrival
date of departure
check-in
security check
accompanied baggage declaration
boarding
Boarding- pass
Travel credit
Travel Insurance
Airspeed
altitude

Plane flight-related terms
Flight ticket
flight reservation
flight timetable
flight schedules
Flight information
Flight delay
flight number
flight path
flight status
flight
flight cancellation
flight cancellation compensation
Flight cancellation refund
Flight cancellation policy
Flight cancellation fees
Flight cancellation charges
3 o'clock flight
Chartered flight
Commercial flight
Connecting flight
Delayed flight
Direct flight
Domestic flight
Evening flight
First flight
Internal flight
Last flight
Lon-distance flight
Morning flight
Night flight
Non-stop flight
Outbound flight
Regular flight
Scheduled flight
Shuttle flight
Special flight

Air transportation-related professions
Pilot
Co-pilot
Air stewardess
Air steward
Flight attendant
Aeronautical engineer
Aerospace engineer
Air traffic controller
Aircraft cleaner
Aircraft designer
Aircraft dispatcher
Aircraft fueler
Aircraft marshaller
Aircraft Mechanic
Aircraft paint technician
Aircraft sheet metal worker
Aircraft upholstery technician
Airline catering service worker
Airline customer service agent
Airline dispatcher
Airline maintenance manager
Airline marketing specialist
Airline operations manager
Airline quality assurance inspector
Airline ramp agent
Airline reservation agent
Airport manager
Airport security officer
Aviation consultant
Aviation journalist
Aviation lawyer
Aviation psychologist
Aviation safety inspector
Avionics technician
Baggage handler
Cargo handler
Flight engineer

Car related verbs
Accelerate (a car)
Align (a car)
balance (car wheels)
brake (a car)
buy (a car)
change (a tyre)
charge (car battery)
check (oil level)
clean (boot)
crash (a car)
design(a car)
Diagnose
drive (a car)
drive-test (a car)
get into (a car)
have(a car)
hire(a car)
install (car electronic device)
insure ((a car)
Jack up (a car)
maintain
overhaul
overtake (a car)
park(a car)
 (a car)
put (petrol)
recalibrate (car sensors)
recharge (car battery)
register(a car)
repair (a car?
Replace (car part)
reverse (a car)
scratch (a car)
sell (a car?
start (a car engine)
tint (car window)
wash (a car)

Road Transport related terms
driving test
driving license
pay fine
suspension of license
speed limit
highway code
speed cameras
breathalyser
a one-way street
lane
left-hand bend
right – hand bend
motorway
highway
parking meter
road sign
yield sign
slip road
traffic jam
traffic congestion
traffic light
roundabout
junction
u-turn
zebra crossing
pedestrian crossing
crossroads
pavement
speed bumps
motorway patrols

Rail transport-related terms
Train station
Railway station
Parking
Transport hubs
Railway depots
Railway yard

In train station
Waiting room
Ticket office
Inquiry office
Information desk
Ticket window
Luggage room
Lost and found
Platform
Rail
Railway tracks
Railway switches
Refreshment room
Information boards
Information displays/ screens
Vending machines
Ticketing systems
Systems for reservation
Wi-Fi and recharging points
First aid service
on the train
Compartment
Sleeper (Sleeping car)
Dining car
Buffet car
Coach class
Car (US)
Carriage (GB)
Seat

Important transportation-related terms
Modes of transportation
Forms of transportation
Means of transport
Mass transit
By land (land transport)
By rail (Rail Transport)
By sea (maritime transport)
By air (air transport)
On foot
Bicycle
motorcycle
car
Bus
Train
Tram
Subway / Metro / Underground
Light rail
Monorail
Cable car
Planes
Pedestrian
Vehicle
spacecraft
Aviation
Logistics
Infrastructure
Roundabout
Traffic
Traffic jam
Traffic congestion
High way
Toll road
Ridesharing
Carpooling
Car renting
Cargo
Automobile

Transport hubs and related places
Bike parking
Bike sharing stations / Bike hire shops
Bus stop
Bus depot
Bus parking
Bus station
Bus terminal
Car parking
Garage/parking lots
Gas station
Petrol station
Taxi rank /stands
Truck terminal /Trucking depots
Subway / Metro stations
Train station
Railway station
Railway terminal
High-speed rail station
Railway depot
Rapid transit stations
Tram stops
Ferry slips
Ferry terminals
Harbour
Seaports/ports
Ship dock
Barge slip
Water taxi rank
Airfield
Airport /airdrome
Hangar/air dock
Spaceports
Intermodal transportation centres
Travel information centre
Logistics and distribution centre
Highway rest areas.

Road and Rail Transport-related Professions
<u>Road transport Professions</u>
Passengers
Chauffeur
Taxi driver
Bus driver
Truck drivers
Delivery driver
Transport planner
logistics coordinators
Roadside assistance technician
driving instructors
Road safety inspectors
Conductor
Ticket collector
Traffic warder
Traffic police
mechanic
cyclist
motorist
<u>Rail Transport Professions</u>
Commuter
Conductor
Engine driver
Guard
Rail traffic controller
Railroad engineer
Railway dispatcher
Railway maintenance workers
Railwayman
Railway planner
Railway security office
Railway station manager
Signal maintainer
Track Inspector
Train driver
Locomotive engine driver

ACKNOWLEDGEMENT:
I would like to thank my wife and all the members of our family
for their support and contributions. Thanks also to my students.

These dialogues are only for educational purposes. All names in the
dialogues are fiction and any resemblance to an actual person or
company is purely unintentional. The author made every effort to ensure
that the information in this book was correct at press time and hereby
disclaims any liability to any party for any loss caused by any errors or
omissions.

.<u>My other books:</u>

SOCIAL ENGLISH DIALOGUES (50 Dialogues +1500 phrases)
50 ENGLISH CLASS DIALOGUES (Discussion topics +wordlist)
50 ENGLISH DIALOGUES (Shopping dialogues + 500 phrases)

Thanks for buying my books and also for your reviews.